Cities through Time

Daily Life in Ancient and Modern

JERUSALEM

by Diane Slavik

illustrations by Ray Webb

RP

Runestone Press/Minneapolis
An imprint of Lerner Publishing Group

The *Cities through Time* series is produced by Runestone Press, an imprint of Lerner Publishing Group, in cooperation with Greenleaf Publishing, Inc., Geneva, Illinois.

Cover design by Michael Tacheny
Text design by Melanie Lawson and Jean DeVaty

Runestone Press
An imprint of Lerner Publishing Group
241 First Avenue North
Minneapolis, Minnesota 55401 U.S.A.

Website address: www.lernerbooks.com

Library of Congress Cataloging-in-Publication Data

Slavik, Diane.
     Daily life in ancient and modern Jerusalem / by Diane Slavik ; illustrations by Ray Webb.
          p.   cm. — (Cities through time)
     Includes index.
     Summary: Explores everyday life in Jerusalem, from the time of the city's founding through Biblical times and the Middle Ages up to the present.
          ISBN 0-8225-3218-2 (lib. bdg. : alk. paper)
     1. Jerusalem—History—Juvenile literature. 2. Jerusalem—Social life and customs—Juvenile literature. [1. Jerusalem.] I. Webb, Ray, ill.
II. Title. III. Series.
DS109.9.C76   2001
956.94'42—dc21   99-042574

Manufactured in the United States of America
2 3 4 5 6 7 – JR – 07 06 05 04 03 02

Contents

Jerusalem's shrine, the Dome of the Rock, is a centerpiece of the city. The reflection of perpetual sunlight on Jerusalem's yellow stone buildings has earned the city the name "Jerusalem the Golden."

Introduction

Jerusalem sits on a hilltop in the southern Judean Hills. The city's setting is a dramatic combination of cliffs and valleys, heights and depths. In ancient times, the area was covered with oaks and pines and was home to a variety of wildlife, even lions.

The Mediterranean Sea lies thirty miles west of Jerusalem. On the city's eastern side, the landscape gradually descends toward the Judean Desert in steps a mile or two wide. At the edge of the desert lies the Dead Sea, the lowest place on the earth's surface. The desert has an average rainfall of twenty-eight inches per year, all of which falls from October to April. During this time, grasses, weeds, and flowers sprout, only to be consumed by the hot, dry summer months of May to September.

Jerusalem sits at the edge of the Fertile Crescent, a region of the Middle East that has been home to many great civilizations since ancient times. Jerusalem's location near the Mediterranean Sea has linked the city to the various cultures of the region. Throughout history, different empires have seized control of Jerusalem in attempts to dominate overland trade routes connecting Asia, Africa, and Europe.

Jerusalem's importance to three world religions—Judaism, Islam, and Christianity—has made it a sacred city to many people. As the seat of the ancient Jewish kingdom, Jerusalem is Judaism's holiest city. The birthplace of Christianity, Jerusalem is also holy to Christians. And as one of the three holy cities of Islam, Jerusalem is revered by Muslims. Because so many peoples consider Jerusalem their own, the city remains a site of strife in modern times.

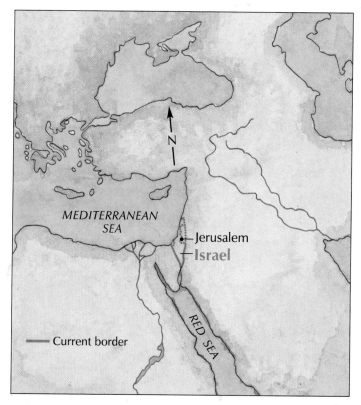

MEDITERRANEAN SEA

Jerusalem

Israel

RED SEA

Current border

Tents to Farms

In ancient times, nomadic shepherds roamed Canaan, the ancient name for the land surrounding Jerusalem. They lived in woolen tents and followed flocks of sheep and goats that grazed in the Judean Desert and the Jerusalem Hills. They carried all of their possessions with them when they traveled.

Historians believe that as these nomads gradually took up farming, they founded small towns throughout Canaan. First called Shalem, Jerusalem may have been one of the towns settled by former Canaanite nomads.

Nomadic families of the region lived a lifestyle that is probably very similar to the lives of nomads in the modern-day Middle East. They lived in large, airy tents, which they made bigger as the family grew. They covered the ground with rugs and cushions. A colorful curtain divided the tent into two halves. Men lived on one side of the tent, while women and children lived on the other.

Baking flat, crispy bread

Goatskin butter churn

The nomads depended on their animals for shelter, clothing, and food. Women spun sheep and goat hair into thread. Using lightweight looms, they wove the thread into cloth, rugs, and tents. Some looms were thirteen yards long. Women also used sheep and goat milk to make yogurt and butter. For yogurt, they boiled the milk, then mixed in a little yogurt from a previous batch. To make butter, they put some yogurt into a goatskin bag, which they hung from a tripod. They rocked the bag until the yogurt turned into butter. Women baked flat, crackerlike bread on metal trays over a fire. Dried dates made tasty snacks.

From 3000 to 2300 B.C., many nomads became farmers. By 2000 B.C., Jerusalem was one of a string of inland cities that linked Egypt in the west to Mesopotamia (modern-day Iraq) in the east. Visiting merchants traded items such as tools and jewelry for weapons. Jerusalem's artisans made the weapons from bronze mined in Canaan.

Nomads depended on their flocks for everything from food to shelter and clothing.

7

A Trade Center

The powerful civilizations of Egypt, Mesopotamia, and Anatolia (in modern-day Turkey) dominated Canaan. At times Jerusalem was heavily taxed or caught up in wars between these cultures. But usually traders passing between the rich cities of these regions found Jerusalem to be a useful trading market, a resting place, and a watering hole.

Jerusalem in 1000 B.C. was similar to the other Canaanite cities. Its dry, hilly land was good for growing barley, a grain that people ground into flour. Wheat was harder to grow, so wheat bread was considered a luxury. Women baked bread in a clay oven shared by several families. People ate lentils, chickpeas, grapes, figs, dates, apricots, and pomegranates. Olive trees dotted the hills. People picked olives, which they ate and crushed to make olive oil. Olive oil was used in cooking, as well as in medicine, in perfumes, and as lamp fuel.

Women raised children, collected water, and helped with farming. Children helped tend the flocks of sheep and goats. Men were farmers, shepherds, merchants, or artisans. Artisans hammered metal, shaped clay into pottery, and carved musical instruments. Jerusalem's natural water source—the Gihon spring—was the center of city life. Women gathered here to socialize and to fill up their clay jugs with water for their households.

Jerusalem's hilltop location gave its residents a good view of approaching trouble. The city walls kept it safe from invaders and wild animals, such as boars, wolves, bears, and lions. Inside the walls, small houses lined winding streets. Some houses centered on courtyards, where people kept animals at night. Large extended families shared homes. The people of Jerusalem worshiped gods of the earth, water, harvest, weather, animals, and the sun. Many people had small religious shrines in their homes.

The city's hills were covered with olive trees and barley fields.

After 1000 B.C., people learned to drill through limestone down to the water table under the earth's surface. They began to collect rainwater in large plaster tanks. People no longer needed to live next to a spring.

Bread baked in clay ovens.

Artisans hammer metal pots.

In this fifteenth-century image *(above)*, Israelite forces clash with the neighboring Philistine army. The Ark of the Covenant *(left)* was covered with gold and carried on poles inserted in rings at the Ark's four lower corners.

Israelites Capture Jerusalem

By the middle of the eleventh century B.C., people known as the Israelites settled in Canaan. They lived in tribal communities to the north and south of Jerusalem. Farmers and shepherds, the Israelites had lived as nomads before settling in Canaan.

Another culture—the Philistines—lived along the Mediterranean coast. When they began to expand their control of the region, violent skirmishes erupted between the Philistines and the Israelites. The Philistines had iron weapons that gave them an advantage over the Israelites, who had weaker bronze weapons.

To face the threat, the Israelites united their tribes and chose kings to lead them. Under King David, the Israelites drove the Philistines back to the coast. Jerusalem lay between the lands of the southern and northern Israelite tribes.

Around 1000 B.C., King David conquered Jerusalem as the capital for his new kingdom of Israel. The Israelites worshiped one god, not many gods. They considered themselves protected by God and believed that they had to follow his laws.

With Jerusalem as the capital of Israel, King David installed the Israelites' most sacred shrine in a tent inside the city. The shrine was called the Ark of the Covenant. The Ark was a rectangular box made of acacia wood and covered in gold. The lid held two cherubs (angels) with outspread wings.

The Ark housed the Ten Commandments—laws God was said to have given to Moses, a biblical leader who led the Israelite tribes from slavery in Egypt to freedom in Canaan. The people believed that the Ark marked the presence of God. The covenant was viewed as a two-way promise between God and the Israelites. The Israelites would worship only God, and God would rule over them with mercy, forgiveness, and love.

King David's Jerusalem had a population of about three thousand. Like other cities of the time, its landscape was dominated by a palace surrounded by housing for the king's staff and soldiers.

In his new capital city, King David bought a piece of land on Mount Moriah. On this property was a large, flat rock used as a threshing floor—a place where people beat stalks of wheat to get the grain. David placed the Ark on this rock, which became the holiest place for the Israelites.

King Solomon's Temple

When King David died, he left his son Solomon a secure kingdom. The new kingdom grew in population and wealth. King Solomon taxed the camel caravans that passed through Israel from Egypt to Mesopotamia. He ordered 1,400 war chariots built and appointed skilled horsemen to drive them. He imported horses from Asia Minor (modern-day Turkey), had them trained, and sold them to Egypt. In fact, Solomon's horses lived in stone stables fancier than the homes of most people.

Solomon constructed a luxurious palace complex where he lived in splendor. He was said to have seven hundred wives. Many belonged to the royal families of other small kingdoms. Solomon married the women in order to keep Israel at peace with its neighbors. He built shrines to honor the gods of his foreign wives.

One of King Solomon's greatest achievements was the construction of a splendid temple that housed the Ark of the Covenant. He chose the site of King David's Temple. The Temple was a marvel of cedar beams, bronze pillars, ivory-paneled doors, golden vessels, and carved stone ornaments. Solomon hired skilled Phoenicians (people from the Mediterranean coast of modern-day Syria and Lebanon) to help build the Temple. Local workers and Phoenicians carved stone. They mined, casted, and hammered copper, bronze, silver, and gold. Only the high priest could enter the double doors leading to the sanctuary, called the Holy of Holies, where the Ark of the Covenant rested. In front of the Temple, steps led to a large bronze altar where priests sacrificed animals. Each of Israel's twelve districts paid food, olive oil, wine, cattle, or grain for the upkeep of the Temple and the palace.

Israel split after Solomon's death. Israel's ten northern districts (each inhabited by one tribe) founded a separate country, Israel, with Samaria as the capital. The other two tribes kept Jerusalem as the capital and called their country Judea.

Brazen Sea basin

At the dedication ceremony for Solomon's Temple, a large number of priests sacrificed as many as 22,000 oxen and 120,000 sheep. In the temple forecourt, twelve huge bronze bulls supported a massive water-filled basin, known as the Brazen Sea, used for ritual cleansing.

Two human-headed lions with wings guarded the inner Holy of Holies.

Wheeled bronze basins were used to wash offerings.

Two pillars called Jachin and Boaz flanked the front doors, which were made of gold inlaid olive wood.

Sacrifices and Celebrations

A nimal sacrifice played an important role in ancient Judaism, as in many ancient religions. People believed that animal sacrifice was a way to make up for sins and to express thanks for meat, leather, and other animal products. Families regularly brought an animal to Solomon's Temple for sacrifice. A poor family might bring a pair of birds, while a more well-to-do family might bring a ram. Priests bled the animal, then they burned certain parts of it. People believed that the animal's living soul returned to its maker in a pillar of sweet-smelling smoke. The family and priests cooked and ate the remaining meat.

Within three hundred years of Solomon's death, the Temple was the only place where Jews performed sacrifices. Judeans celebrated festivals to mark the seasons. Passover, held each spring, was a time to thank God for large flocks and for the Jews' freedom in Israel and Judea. Most people owned animals. Sheep were important to life in those times. Poorer families might share one flock among them, thus sharing the work and cost of feeding and housing the animals. At Passover each family brought a lamb to be sacrificed at the Temple.

After the sacrifice of the animal at the Temple, the family returned home with a portion of the meat. There they reenacted the last night in Egypt before Moses led the Israelite people to freedom. The father dipped a sprig of marjoram (an herb) in a bowl filled with the sacrificial lamb's blood and swabbed the doorway of the home. This recalled the biblical story of how God killed the firstborn son in every Egyptian house except those in homes marked as belonging to Israelites. After sundown, the family roasted and ate the lamb. They also ate crackerlike unleavened bread because their fleeing ancestors hadn't had time to let the bread rise before they baked it. They ate bitter herbs to remind them of the bitter years of their ancestors' slavery.

Now the bronze pillars which were in
the house of the Lord, and the stands
and the bronze sea which were in the
house of the Lord, the Chaldeans
broke in pieces and carried the bronze
to Babylon. And they took away the
pots, the shovels, the snuffers, the
spoons, and all the bronze vessels
which were used in temple service. The
captain of the guard also took away
the firepans and the basins, what was
fine gold and what was fine silver. The
two pillars, the one sea, and the
stands which Solomon had made for
the house of the Lord—the bronze of
all these vessels was beyond weight.
 —II Kings 25:13-16,
New American Standard Bible

Jerusalem Is Destroyed

In 722 B.C., the Assyrians conquered Israel. Later, in 701 B.C., the Assyrians laid siege to Jerusalem. Laying siege to a town meant surrounding it with soldiers and barriers. This kept the townspeople inside and all possible help out. The town could be starved into surrender. The Assyrians finally turned from the city, but they taxed the lands around Judea and controlled the trade routes.

Judea soon faced another threat. The Chaldeans of Babylon, under King Nebuchadnezzar (who ruled from around 605 B.C. to 562 B.C.), began to expand their territory. In 597 B.C., after a long, terrible siege, the Chaldeans broke through the walls of Jerusalem. They laid waste to the city and destroyed the Temple. The Ark of the Covenant disappeared. Many people died, and most survivors were exiled to Babylon. King Nebuchadnezzar believed that exiling people from their land made them less likely to rebel. Others—mainly poor farmers—stayed behind.

The Persian Empire (based in what would become Iran) conquered Babylon in 539 B.C. Persia's King Cyrus decreed that people exiled by the Chaldeans could return to their homelands. Many Jews chose to remain in Babylon, where they had prospered.

Some Jews returned to Jerusalem. Those returning spoke Aramaic, a language spoken in Babylon. The Jews' native Hebrew became the language of religious worship.

The residents of Jerusalem were new immigrants and descendants of the Jews who had stayed. Many were wary of the newcomers from Babylon. The new arrivals were shocked to find Jerusalem crumbling. Weeds choked the city's paths. The city walls—an important defense—lay in ruins from the Chaldean destruction. In 445 B.C., Jerusalem's governor organized the city's families to rebuild their city. It was slow and discouraging labor, but the people of Jerusalem worked to help in the effort. Slowly, Jerusalem's condition improved. Eventually, more people returned from Babylon and constructed a new Temple.

The Chaldeans pillage Solomon's Temple (*above left*), destroying the enormous columns and the Brazen Sea basin. In Rembrandt's portrait (*left*), the seventh-century B.C. prophet Jeremiah weeps for his demolished homeland.

Life in Greek Jerusalem

In 332 B.C., the Greek emperor Alexander the Great marched triumphantly into Jerusalem. He made Judea part of his expanding Greek Empire, which had defeated the Persian Empire.

Alexander gave the Jews political and religious freedom. Many Greek soldiers married women from Jerusalem. After the death of Alexander the Great in 323 B.C., his empire split into kingdoms. Jerusalem came under the rule of the Seleucid dynasty (family of rulers).

Trade with cities from Egypt to Macedonia (northern Greece) brought a flood of new goods into the city. Trade caravans brought slaves, incense, pottery, jewels, and wheat. Greek artisans, scholars, and traders flocked to Jerusalem. People spoke Greek. The people of Jerusalem learned about Greek art, architecture, philosophy, and education.

The young men of Jerusalem attended Greek schools, which worked to improve the body and the mind. At the schools, the young men also competed in athletic events. They had the chance to study Greek philosophy and read Greek epics, such as Homer's *Iliad*. The Greek way of life embraced open discussion and problem solving. This was a drastic shift from traditional education in Jerusalem, which focused on learning religious laws.

In reaction to the Greek cultural influence, Jewish people formed separate groups, including the Pharisees, the Sadducees, and the Essenes. Some Jews chose to continue to closely follow the traditional Jewish laws to avoid the influence of Greek culture. Others welcomed Greek ways and did not believe that the new ideas would hurt Judaism.

Alexander the Great is depicted rushing into battle in a second-century mosaic *(left)*. In a Renaissance-era painting *(above)*, Alexander meets with his advisers inside the rebuilt Temple.

The Essenes have a reputation for cultivating peculiar sanctity....They shun pleasures as a vice and regard temperance and the control of the passions as a special virtue....Riches they despise, and their community of goods is truly admirable; you will not find one among them distinguished by greater opulence than another....

The Pharisees, who are considered the most accurate interpreters of the laws, and hold the position of the leading sect, attribute everything to Fate and to God; they hold that to act rightly or otherwise rests, indeed, for the most part with men, but that in each action Fate cooperates....The Sadducees, on the contrary, are, even among themselves, rather boorish in their behavior, and in their intercourse with their peers are as rude as to aliens. Such is what I have to say on the Jewish philosophical schools.

—Josephus, ancient Jewish historian

All members of the family worked hard to prepare for the Sabbath, the weekly day of rest.

The Torah

Most Jews in Greek Jerusalem followed rules of eating, cleanliness, and observing holy days as set down in the Torah, the first five books of their holy scripture. The 613 rules and teachings in the Torah covered every aspect of daily life.

According to the Torah, certain foods were kosher (clean). All plants were kosher. Pork and shellfish were never kosher. No meat was kosher unless the butcher prepared it a certain way. People kept meat and milk products separate. To make this possible, kitchens had two separate areas—one for meat and one for milk products.

Special rules of cleanliness—called purity laws—applied to people, too. People who had diseases, women who had just given birth, and people who had touched the dead were considered unclean. But they could be purified. Some Jewish pilgrims (religious travelers) had to be purified in Jerusalem. They waited seven days (some might have to wait as long as eighty days) before visiting the Temple. On the third and seventh days, they bathed in ashes and running water, not water pulled from a well. The walls were posted with signs that threatened death to visitors to the Temple who didn't follow the rules. Some very religious Jews tried to follow these rules closely so they were always ready for Temple worship.

The Torah required a Sabbath, a weekly day of rest. The Sabbath began on Friday at sunset and lasted until the first star appeared Saturday evening. Strict followers of Sabbath rules—as well as their animals, and their servants—did no work of any kind on that day. No cooking, cleaning, spinning, weaving, or handling of money was allowed. To prepare for the Sabbath, the women of the household prepared all the meals in advance. After a special family meal on Friday evening, the rest of the Sabbath was spent resting, socializing, and going to the Temple.

21

Jerusalem Becomes a Roman City

The Seleucids warred with other Greek kingdoms. Meanwhile the Roman Empire gradually rose in power. Roman forces broke through the walls of Jerusalem in 63 B.C., and a Roman governor became the ruler of Jerusalem. Roman civil law became the law of the land, and Roman soldiers walked the streets of Jerusalem.

In 37 B.C., the Roman general Mark Antony appointed Herod, a Jew, to be king of Judea. Herod—who became known as Herod the Great—owed allegiance and taxes to Rome but was otherwise free to run his kingdom as he saw fit. He had workers build an amphitheater and a theater. In about 20 B.C., Herod began remodeling the Temple and the sanctuary. The size and shape of the sanctuary could not be changed because of specific biblical instructions, but it could be made even more beautiful.

Herod trained one thousand priests as masons and carpenters to work on the holiest sections of the Temple. Work on the sanctuary was completed in a year and a half. Vines and fruit made of gold decorated the entrance.

About eighteen thousand laborers worked on the rest of the structure. Masons quarried, cut, and transported massive blocks of stone to create a level, thirty-five-acre platform supported by thick walls. The average stone weighed between two and ten tons. The largest was as heavy as 415 tons. Stonemasons fitted

From a distance, the gold on the Temple *"reflected so fierce a blaze of fire that those who tried to look at it were forced to turn away."*
—Josephus, ancient Jewish historian and eyewitness to the Roman destruction of Jerusalem

Herod the Great remodeled Jerusalem's Temple (*above*).

the stones together so precisely that not even a knife blade could pass between them. After eleven years, the new structure glittered white and gold above the city. But work continued for seventy more years. Signs in Greek and Latin were posted on the walls, warning non-Jewish visitors to keep away from the sacred Temple. But a portion of the platform was left open to everyone. There visitors could exchange foreign money and find courts of justice. At Jerusalem's nearby marketplace, people could buy or sell almost anything.

Daily Life under Herod

In Roman Jerusalem, two-story stone houses crowded next to each other or even shared outer walls. Most streets were narrow and twisted around houses. Almost every house enclosed a small, open-air patio. Inside the homes, artisans painted beautiful flowers and patterns on the plaster-covered walls of the rooms. Tile mosaics covered some floors. Most houses had flat roofs where families often ate and where visitors could sleep.

People ate bread made from barley, which women ground into flour at home. Bread was cooked in small cylindrical ovens. Fish, pigeons, and stews made with lamb or beans were hearty meals. Butter and cheese were made from goat's milk. Cooks used honey for sweetening. For a treat, people nibbled on cooked grasshoppers.

Several generations shared houses. In wealthy homes, slaves did most of the work, but wives spun, wove, and sewed. Wives did all of the housework, cooking, shopping, and child-rearing in most other homes.

Under King Herod, a religious education program was started. Beginning at age five, boys learned to read the Torah. By age thirteen, when school ended, most boys knew the scriptures by heart. Girls didn't attend school. Instead, they learned how to run a house, spin, weave, and tend animals.

Parents usually had many children. When a child entered his or her early teens, parents arranged a future marriage. A year of betrothal (engagement) followed, when the two families haggled over the bride's dowry, an amount of money or goods that the bride's family could afford to give the groom's family.

Children played with toys such as balls, tops, and hoops.

Flat rooftops were handy for sleeping and entertaining.

Most men had one wife, but more than one was allowed. A husband could divorce his wife for any reason, such as not bearing children. A divorced woman needed her ex-husband's permission to remarry.

Girls usually helped tend the family animals.

Straw, dry grass, or charcoal fueled stoves.

25

Crucifixion, a Roman method of execution, was a brutal practice. The condemned man was typically whipped and forced to carry a heavy crossbar to his place of execution. Once the cross was in place, soldiers stripped the criminal and pinned him to the cross by hammering long nails through his limbs. Unable to breathe easily, the victim usually died of suffocation.

Jesus addresses an attentive crowd *(above)*. People gather to watch the crucifixion of a condemned man named Adoni-Bezek, who was crucified without the use of nails *(right)*.

Tense Times in Jerusalem

Crimes were harshly punished in Roman-controlled Jerusalem. The punishment for murder, robbery, and rebellion was crucifixion—being nailed to a wooden cross and left to die. Rows of crude wooden crosses began to appear on the outskirts of town, warning of the penalty inflicted on those who defied Roman laws. To let people know why the person had been condemned, a card listing the person's crimes was attached to the cross.

In the Roman system of justice, local chief priests or religious elders brought charges against a person. Crowds of onlookers were free to express their opinions. Trials did not involve juries. A Roman procurator (governor), who passed sentence, oversaw the trials.

Roman rulers allowed people to follow their own religions as long as they publicly took part in important Roman religious rituals, including sacrifices to the Roman god Jupiter. But many Jews refused, which Roman rulers considered to be rebellion.

Meanwhile, Jewish pilgrims continued traveling to the Temple to worship. For the Jewish festivals of Passover, Shavuoth, and Sukkoth, many thousands of pilgrims poured into the city. They stayed in synagogues (Jewish places of worship), private homes, or camped in the nearby hills. Roman authorities worked hard to control the large crowds.

A Jewish man named Jesus lived during these turbulent times. He preached in Galilee, an area in Judea. Jesus believed that devotion to God meant sharing in God's love for one's neighbors. Like some other Jews, Jesus did not believe in extremely strict Jewish practice. Jesus claimed to be a messiah (savior), one who would eventually bring salvation to the world. Some people strongly disapproved of his message. Others embraced it.

Jesus gained powerful enemies. At Passover he went to Jerusalem, where he was arrested. He was brought before a procurator. He was accused of claiming to be the King of the Jews and promising the Jews a new kingdom. This charge concerned Roman authorities. Since Archelaus, King Herod's son, had died, no king had been found to succeed him. (Archelaus ruled from A.D. 4 until he was deposed in A.D. 6.)

Jesus was tried, convicted of treason, and executed by crucifixion. Jesus' followers believed that he returned from the dead three days later and was soon carried up to heaven. After these events, Jesus' followers spread Jesus' message. In time, Christianity became a separate religion.

The Romans...massacred indiscriminately all whom they met, and burnt the houses with all who had taken refuge within. Often in the course of their raids, on entering the houses for loot, they would find whole families dead and the rooms filled with the victims of the famine, and then, shuddering at the sight, retire empty-handed. Yet, while they pitied those who had thus perished, they had no similar feelings for the living, but, running everyone through who fell in their way, they choked the alleys with corpses and deluged the whole city with blood....

—Josephus

The Roman general Titus leads his army in destroying the Temple of Jerusalem, massacring people in his way.

Rebellion and Destruction

In A.D. 66, a Roman governor, who was under pressure to pay heavy taxes to Rome, tried to take money from the Temple's bank. When the Jews rebelled in a bloody clash, the Roman general Titus besieged Jerusalem. After years of trouble with rebels in Jerusalem, this rebellion was the last straw. The Romans destroyed the city's walls with a battering ram.

Titus and his soldiers leveled much of Jerusalem, including the Temple and much of the platform. Of the Temple, only the western section of the platform's retaining wall still stood. The Romans sent prisoners to amphitheaters in the eastern reaches of the empire, where they were killed before cheering spectators. In the amphitheaters, some prisoners died in forced combat, some were killed by wild beasts, and some were burned alive. Other people were condemned to forced labor. Prisoners were forced to work in Egyptian mines, build the Roman Coliseum, and dig canals in Corinth. Many Roman soldiers settled in Jerusalem, but most other people deserted the city.

The Roman emperor Hadrian arrived in Jerusalem in A.D. 130. He wanted to build a new Roman city to replace the ruined Jerusalem. He planned a temple to the Roman god Jupiter that would rest on Temple Mount. This plan was intolerable to the remaining Jews, who in 132 rose up against Rome. When the rebellion failed, the Jews were banned from Jerusalem. The name Jerusalem was erased by an imperial order. The new city built on the ruins was named Aelia Capitolina—but the name didn't stick. Hadrian also changed the region's name from Judea to Palaestina (Palestine), a word still in use in modern times.

Aelia Capitolina

After Hadrian banned the Jews, Jerusalem became home to Egyptian, Arabian, and Phoenician settlers. Most people followed Egyptian or Roman religious practices. Christianity was against the law. Followers of the new religion Christianity practiced their faith in secret. Viewing Christians as troublemakers, Roman authorities executed some for their faith.

Then in 313, the Roman emperor Constantine made Christianity an official religion of the Roman Empire. Constantine's mother, Queen Helena, made a pilgrimage to Jerusalem to visit places Jesus had been. Jerusalem soon had shrines at locations Christians associated with Jesus' last days. Early Christians stopped to pray at holy places along the Via Dolorosa (Walk of Sorrow), the path Jesus walked to his crucifixion. Constantine built a magnificent church, called the Church of the Resurrection, to enclose what followers believed to be Jesus' tomb. Situated at the end of the Via Dolorosa, the Church of the Resurrection was the holiest spot of all.

Nuns and priests built convents and monasteries in Jerusalem and in the hills around the city. Jerusalem became the site of much new building. A *cardo* (a wide street paved with very large stones) ran through the middle of Jerusalem. A row of stone columns lined the entire length of the cardo on both sides, separating pedestrians from the horses, camels, and donkeys pulling carts. The columns were linked to shops by a roof that shaded shoppers from the hot sun. Merchants spread their goods on tables in the shade.

Pilgrims in a fifteenth-century relief *(above)* are given a hospitable welcome upon arriving in Jerusalem. This fourteenth-century manuscript illumination *(left)* shows pilgrims making the long, uncomfortable, and often dangerous trip to the holy city.

The Holy Rock, Jerusalem

A Quiet Invasion

In 571 an Arab named Muhammad was born in Mecca, a city in what would become Saudi Arabia. He founded a new religion, Islam, whose followers are called Muslims. They founded a huge empire that, in time, stretched across North Africa and encompassed the modern-day Middle East. In 638 a caliph (successor to Muhammad) named Omar invaded Jerusalem. After a long siege, Muslim forces peacefully took charge of the city.

Omar declared that Christians and Jews should be free to worship in their own way. Jews were even allowed back into the city to live. The members of each religion lived separately. A Jewish community formed south of Temple Mount. Muslims settled near the Temple platform. Christians—who made up most of the city's population—clustered near the Church of the Resurrection.

As the Islamic Empire grew in wealth, Caliph Abd al-Malik built a shrine (Muslim house of worship) on the site of the destroyed Temple. Architects and skilled workers from Constantinople (modern-day Istanbul) and Armenia created a splendid structure topped with a gold-covered lead dome.

The shrine became known as the Dome of the Rock. The shrine surrounds the threshing stone purchased by King David in ancient times. According to the Koran, the Bible, and the Torah (the sacred books of each religion), the boulder has special religious significance. Over time the population of Jerusalem became almost entirely Muslim.

Muslim worshipers *(left)* kneel before the Holy Rock housed within a shrine called the Dome of the Rock. When they pray, Muslims face the direction of the holy city of Mecca (in modern-day Saudi Arabia).

The Five Pillars of Islam

Many Muslims compare Islam to a strong building held up by five pillars. The Five Pillars are:

1. Allah (God) is the only god, and Muhammad is God's prophet.
2. Every Muslim should pray five times a day.
3. Muslims should give to the poor.
4. Muslims should fast each year during the month of Ramadan.
5. Muslims should make a pilgrimage to the holy city of Mecca at least once in their lifetime.

> *In the name of Allah, the merciful,*
> *the compassionate.*
> *Allah is most great. I witness that*
> *there is no god but Allah.*
> *I witness that Muhammad is Allah's*
> *Prophet.*
> *Come to prayers. Come and be saved.*
> *Allah is most great. There is no Allah*
> *but Allah.*
>
> —A Muslim prayer recited five
> times a day to call people to prayer

Worish at a Mosque

The mosque was a center of life for Muslims in Jerusalem. Not only did it provide an important place to worship Allah, it also served as a gathering place for Muslim men. All mosques had at least one tower called a minaret. A muezzin (crier) climbed the tower and called people to prayer five times a day. Muslims stopped what they were doing and said their prayers.

Wherever mosques were built, they became centers of local life. They were places where many people worked and where friends and neighbors met at least once a week. Community leaders gathered there at the end of Friday prayers to discuss local issues.

Before entering the mosque, worshipers removed their shoes. They washed their hands, face, arms, and feet at a large fountain in the mosque's courtyard. Inside the mosque was a large open room without an altar or furniture. People stood and then knelt on the floor, which was covered with beautiful carpets. Worshipers also brought individual prayer rugs. At one end of the mosque, a small ornate alcove called a *mihrab* showed worshipers the direction of Mecca, toward which they faced to pray. A stairway led to a small platform or pulpit, called the *minbar*.

On Friday, the holy day to Muslims, men went to the mosque for midday prayers. The person who led prayers was called an imam. Each prayer lasted about ten minutes. After prayers, men listened to preaching from the minbar. Men covered their heads as a sign of respect to God. Women and girls usually prayed at home. If they came to a mosque, they prayed in a private gallery or behind screens. In modern times, Muslim worshipers follow these same customs.

Exquisite painted tiles covered the walls of most mosques. No pictures of people or animals were permitted in a mosque, so artists often decorated the tiles with ornately written verses from the Koran.

A 1910 painting depicts Jerusalem's Mosque of Omar *(left)*. A trio of Muslim men face Mecca at dawn for the first of their five daily prayers *(above)*.

Crusader Life

In 1095 Pope Urban II (leader of the Roman Catholic Church) urged knights to volunteer to capture Jerusalem. The pope believed that Jerusalem should be controlled by Christians instead of Muslims. Soon twenty-six thousand foot soldiers and four thousand knights set out from France to conquer the city.

In June 1099, the long, grueling journey ended as the Crusaders arrived in Jerusalem. Equipped with armor and riding large, sturdy horses, the knights seemed invincible. With only one thousand soldiers to defend the city, the Muslim caliph wanted a truce, but the Crusaders refused. After a month of siege, the Crusaders conquered the city, killing so many men, women, and children that the streets and alleys were red with blood.

Victorious, the Crusaders founded the Kingdom of Jerusalem. They rebuilt the Church of the Resurrection and named it the Church of the Holy Sepulcher. They took charge of estates and moved into large, luxurious villas. The Crusaders were amazed by the quality of the decorations, carpets, furniture, and porcelain they found. They tasted foods not found in Europe, such as apricots, figs, sugar, and lemons. They exchanged their heavy wool clothes for cotton and silk.

The master of a Crusader estate worked to defend the Kingdom of Jerusalem. He also hunted for meat and managed the estate's servants. The master's wife cooked, brewed beer, made wine, and sewed clothes. Many Muslims from the local population worked for the Crusaders as farmers, cooks, housekeepers, and nursemaids.

The sons of Crusaders trained to become knights. At age seven, a boy became a page with many duties, such as serving the table at mealtimes. At fourteen, a boy became a squire who trained for battle and learned archery. Girls helped with cooking, sewing, embroidery, weaving, and playing music. Both boys and girls learned to play chess. Some young people learned to read.

One hundred years after the Crusaders arrived, Saladin, a Kurdish ruler of the Islamic Empire, conquered Jerusalem. Saladin's line continued in power until 1260, when the Mamluks of Egypt won control of the Islamic Empire. By 1291 Palestine was in Muslim hands. The fortunes of Jerusalem greatly improved. The Mamluks built a new commercial center on the site of an old Crusader market. People manufactured soap, cotton, and linen products, which attracted new foreign trade.

In this fifteenth-century illuminated manuscript, Jerusalem is looted after its capture by Christian Crusaders in 1099.

Piles of heads, hands, and feet were to be seen in the streets of the city. It was necessary to pick one's way over the bodies....Indeed, it was a just and splendid judgment of God, that this place should be filled with the blood of the unbelievers, when it had suffered so long from their blasphemies.

—Raymond of Agiles, an eyewitness to the Crusades

Medieval Pilgrims

Medieval Christians believed that by doing penance (an action to show they were sorry for their sins), God would forgive their sins. Taking the difficult, dangerous trip to Jerusalem was believed to earn a place in heaven for even the worst of sinners. A knight named Fulk the Black traveled from France three times to beg forgiveness for massacring his enemies and murdering his wife. In Jerusalem he asked monks to beat him with branches as he shouted, "Accept, O Lord, the wretched Fulk."

Pilgrims walked across Europe to Venice, a city-state in northeastern Italy. Along the roads, church leaders founded hospices that provided food, shelter, and places to worship. It was a dangerous journey. Thieves set upon some groups, and others got sick from drinking dirty water.

In the spring and fall, boats left Venice for the Holy Land. An average ticket cost about the same as a new horse. Ships sailed to Jaffa, a port on the Mediterranean Sea. There pilgrims paid fees to the Muslims to be allowed to enter Jerusalem. While waiting to leave Jaffa, the pilgrims spent a miserable night in unsanitary caves in Jaffa. Then they set off on a two-day, thirty-nine-mile walk to Jerusalem, accompanied by Muslim guides. Donkeys carried their bags.

Once in the city, pilgrims visited holy

sites, such as the Via Dolorosa. At the Church of the Holy Sepulchre, guards collected entry fees and checked the pilgrims' papers before allowing them to enter. Friars (members of a religious organization sworn to poverty) guided small groups of pilgrims. At Calvary, where Jesus' cross had stood, pilgrims were often overwhelmed. Some fell to the ground and wept with great emotion.

Pilgrims from Europe were shocked to see the poverty of Jerusalem. By the 1480s, only about four thousand families lived in the city. The seventy or so Jewish families in Jerusalem could practice their own religion. But they had to pay crushing fees to the Muslim rulers to do ordinary things, such as build new homes.

(Opposite) Christian pilgrims visit the Church of the Holy Sepulchre, guarded by Muslims. *(Above)* Pilgrims bathe in the Jordan River at the spot where John the Baptist baptized Jesus.

Wey's *Itineraries*, a popular fifteenth-century tour guide, gave pilgrims valuable information, such as: *"When you come to haven towns, if you shall* [stay] *there three days, go* [immediately] *to land to secure lodging ahead of the others, for it will be taken quickly, and, if there is any good food, get it before the others arrive. On arriving at Jaffa, the port of Jerusalem, the same haste must be observed so as to secure one of the best donkeys. You shall pay no more for the best than for the worst."*

Süleyman the Great

From Asia came another group of invaders, known as the Ottomans. This powerful group converted to Islam and took control of the failing Islamic Empire. In 1517 Jerusalem fell to Ottoman control. Süleyman the Great, an Ottoman sultan (ruler) ruled from 1520 to 1566. He made many improvements to the city. Süleyman had workers build and repair pipelines and aqueducts that carried water over long distances into the city. Workers carved pools into the rocky landscape in different parts of the city and built underground tanks, called cisterns, to store water. Süleyman built pools for public bathing and erected schools, mosques, and hospitals.

Süleyman also built a new, magnificent wall around Jerusalem. Seven ornate gates led into the city. Many replaced older gates. The Damascus Gate, in the north, connected to the cardo, the old Roman market street. The Jaffa Gate, in the west, brought pilgrims and goods into town

Islamic law divided food into three different groups. *Halal* foods—such as fish, fruit, grain, vegetables, and foods considered **kosher** by the Jews—were permitted. *Makruh* foods could be eaten but were not encouraged. *Haram* foods, such as pork and the meat of carnivorous animals, were forbidden. Alcohol and drugs were also haram.

At right, Ottoman soldiers guard the Temple of Jerusalem for their leader, Süleyman the Great *(left)*.

from the Mediterranean port of Jaffa. In the wide open space outside these gates, traders rested their donkeys or camels and unloaded their goods after their journey to Jerusalem.

At the souk (market), shoppers could find almost anything. The markets appeared to be disorganized and overflowing, but they actually were set up according to a special design. Sellers grouped similar items together. For example, jewelry and other luxury items were sold inside a building or in a protected area near a mosque. Vendors sold fresh fruits and vegetables near the city's gates.

During the time of Süleyman, schools improved. Boys could continue their education through their teen years. They studied the Koran, grammar, geometry, and astronomy.

Gifted young men had the opportunity to go on to a *medrese* (college). At a medrese, a young man might study philosophy, science, medicine, or law. Some students went on to become scribes (copyists), lawyers, or civil servants. The best students became medrese teachers.

Muslim homes in Jerusalem contained separate sections for men and women.

Ottoman Family Life

Under the Ottoman Empire, most of Jerusalem's population was Muslim. But there were minorities of Christians and Jews, sometimes called *dhimmis* (members of a protected minority). They did not have the same rights as the Muslims, and they paid more in taxes. But dhimmis did have religious freedom.

In Muslim Jerusalem, the family was the most important unit of society. The oldest man led the household. Family members respected mothers because they looked after the health and happiness of their families. Most Muslim households included aunts, uncles, and grandparents living under the same roof. When a couple married, the wife moved into her husband's family home. Large houses had separate sections for men and women. Because Islam permits a man to have up to four wives, women's quarters could be very large.

According to Islam, men had to always be covered from the navel to the knees, even when swimming. Women had to dress modestly. They covered their whole bodies, except for their faces and hands. Dresses were loose fitting. A veil or scarf called a *hijab* was worn over the head.

Many Muslims honor the holy writings of Jews and Christians and include many of the same stories of the prophets, or messengers, in the Koran. According to Islam, Allah sent many prophets to give guidance to people, including biblical figures such as Adam, Noah, Abraham, Moses, and Jesus. Muslims believe that Allah's last and greatest prophet was Muhammad.

Women of the household cooked and wove cloth to make the family's clothes.

Unless guests were present, the rules relaxed at home.

From the age of four, a boy went to a school called a *madrasah*. Boys learned to read and write Arabic and to recite the Koran. They also learned the correct way to pray and how to perform *wudu*, the special washing before prayers. Since ancient times, the very rich had hired teachers for their children. Under the Ottoman Empire, mosques set up schools called *kuttabs*. From the age of seven, Muslim boys could attend these schools for a few years. In addition to continued study of the Koran, boys learned a little poetry and math. Advanced schooling, including lessons at a medrese, was available to the best students. They might study for as long as twenty years. Students went from one master to another. Scholars often traveled to new cities to further their studies. Muhammad had advised, "Search for knowledge, even if you must go to China to find it!"

Some girls attended school or were taught to read by tutors or their parents. Some wealthy women became scholars. Others earned a living by copying the Koran by hand. Girls also learned how to cook, spin thread, and weave cloth.

Decline of the Ottoman Empire

Gradually the Ottoman Empire began to decline. The improvements constructed under Süleyman began to crumble. In the 1800s, Europeans found new interest in Jerusalem. Many began to look for historical sites mentioned in the Bible. Europeans from many countries built monasteries, orphanages, hospitals, schools, synagogues, mosques, and hospices in Jerusalem. They also funded projects such as paving the city's dirt roads, installing kerosene streetlights, and collecting garbage. Workers planted trees along streets, which were regularly sprinkled with water when dust became a problem. A police force and a museum of antiquities were added. Actors performed plays in Arabic, Turkish, and French at a new theater.

Pilgrims from Europe flooded Jerusalem and Palestine. In the 1870s, between ten thousand and twenty thousand pilgrims visited Jerusalem each year. Many Christian pilgrims stayed in the city for five or six months. Although some stayed in monasteries or convents, others stayed at inns run by local residents. Many people in Jerusalem manufactured and exported religious articles, such as rosaries (strings of prayer beads) and crosses. At one time, Jerusalem had seven hundred artisans and merchants. A variety of industries, crafts, and farms quietly prospered.

A new road between Jaffa and Jerusalem, finished in 1869, brought merchants with wood flooring, roof tiles, and other new construction materials into Jerusalem. Jewish immigrants settled on the western end of town, outside the city's ancient walls. By 1910, about forty thousand pilgrims visited the city each year.

New strides in garbage collection improved health and sanitation.

Artisans made small wooden crosses to sell to tourists.

45

Although their families hadn't lived in Jerusalem for generations, Jews around the world remembered their ancient city. In his memoir *Kindheit im Exil (Childhood in Exile),* Shmaryahu Levin, a Russian Jew, recalls how his mother told the story of Jerusalem's destruction. She spoke with so much freshness, passion, and personal indignation "that the sense of time was wholly destroyed," writes Levin. It was as though "we, our family, our relatives and friends had lived in glorious Jerusalem."

Pilgrims and Jewish Settlers

Many Christian pilgrims were older Russians who had pinched and saved all their lives to be able to afford a visit to Jerusalem. On the night before Easter, pilgrims crammed into the Church of the Holy Sepulchre. There was no room to even take a deep breath. Those who fainted had to be lifted out over the heads of the crowd. People even climbed onto the roof to peer down at the worship.

Each person held a wax candle. The church smelled of warm human bodies and incense. The chatter of conversations mixed with droning chants. Occasionally a baby began to cry.

At last, a flame shot out from the tomb in the center of the room where Jesus was believed to have been laid. The priest lit his candle and used it to light someone else's. Soon, every candle burned. Each person carried his or her candle out of the church and used it to light other candles in the city.

In the late 1800s, Jewish people living across Europe were persecuted for their beliefs, especially in Russia. Many Jews

Amid the glow of many candles, pilgrims and other worshipers squeeze into the Church of the Holy Sepulchre on the night before Easter *(left)*. Pedestrians stroll along a street near Jerusalem's Jaffa Gate in the year 1900 *(above)*.

were killed. Synagogues were burned. Many Jewish families left Russia to settle in the United States.

Others became part of the Zionist movement, which urged Jews to move back to their ancient homeland of Palestine. They believed they needed a nation of their own to be safe. This situation soon led to political conflict. Arabs living in Palestine and Jerusalem considered it their home, too.

47

The British Mandate and the Holocaust

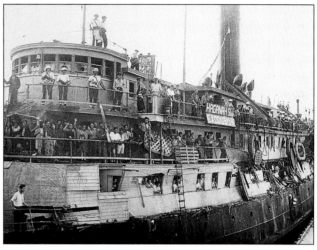

World War I (1914–1918) led to the collapse of the Ottoman Empire. Great Britain, which took charge of Palestine, had a mandate, or authorization, to govern the area until the people of the region could govern themselves independently. Both the Jews and the Muslim Arabs questioned Great Britain's fairness. On one hand, the Arabs had fought alongside the British in World War I. The Arabs had helped the British overthrow the Ottoman Empire. As a result, Great Britain had promised them eventual independence. On the other hand, a 1917 British government document called the Balfour Declaration favored the idea of giving the Jews the right to regain their homeland. The British were unable to keep both promises. Tension and violence became an everyday part of life in Jerusalem.

Events in Europe soon transformed Jerusalem. In the 1930s, Hitler and the Nazi party gained control of Germany, which had a large Jewish population. As the Nazis rose in power, they blamed the Jews for the economic problems the country experienced after World War I. Jews living in territory occupied by the Nazis were first discriminated against and then systematically murdered in concentration camps. After the Nazis were defeated in World War II (1939–1945), the world learned that six million Jews had been murdered. This crime became known as the Holocaust. People around the world began to agree with the Zionists that the Jews deserved a safe homeland. Arabs stated that the crimes of the Holocaust were committed in Europe by Europeans. They did not believe that they should have to pay for these crimes by giving Palestine to the Jews.

A riot erupts at Jerusalem's Jaffa Gate during a revolt against British control of Palestine in 1933 (right). The Jewish liberty ship, the *Exodus*, lands in Israel on July 18, 1947, carrying Jewish refugees seeking a new life (above).

I would clear out everything that is not sacred, set up workers' houses beyond the city, empty and tear down the filthy rat-holes, burn all non-sacred ruins, and put the bazaars elsewhere. Then, retaining as much of the old architectural style as possible, I would build an airy, comfortable, properly sewered, brand new city around the holy places.

—Theodor Herzl,
Zionist champion, 1898

The Two Wars

Great Britain handed control of Palestine to the United Nations (UN) in 1947. The UN decided to divide Palestine into two states. Part of the country came under Jewish rule as the State of Israel. Arab Palestinians retained control of part of the region, called Palestine. The Palestinians outnumbered the Israelis two to one, but Palestine was slightly smaller than Israel. Many Palestinians were angry that they had lost the region's best farmland and Jaffa, an important port on the Mediterranean Sea. They rejected the UN proposal. Because of its religious importance to Christians, Jews, and Muslims, Jerusalem became an international city—controlled by no single nation and open to everyone.

On May 14, 1948, Israel declared itself a nation. The next day, five neighboring Arab states launched the Palestine War, hoping to claim Israel for the Palestinians. By the end of the year, Israel won the war and enlarged its territory. Some Palestinians moved to neighboring Arab countries, some became Israeli citizens, and some lived in UN camps outside Israel's borders.

Between 1948 and 1967, Jerusalem was divided into two sections. Palestinians lived on the eastern side where most holy sites, including the Western Wall, were

found. The Jews lived on the western side. A barbed wire fence ran through the gutted houses and deserted streets that separated the two sides.

In 1966 and 1967, Egypt and other nearby nations led attacks on Israel. In 1967 Israeli forces responded by attacking Syria, Jordan, Iraq, and Egypt. In the Six-Day War (so called because it lasted for only six days), the Israelis captured territory near their borders. They declared that all of Jerusalem was part of Israel.

Arab refugees leave Jerusalem in 1948 to find a more stable home *(opposite)*. Israeli soldiers pray at the Western Wall, a holy site, in 1967 for the first time in 19 years *(below)*.

These were years of fear and nostalgia on both sides. Pious Jews gazed from their rooftops, across minefields, toward the lost stones where they could no longer worship. Arabs, likewise, stared across in the opposite direction at the old homes in West Jerusalem they had been forced to abandon during the fighting, which were now occupied by new Jewish immigrants. In daytime, snipers lay in wait behind sandbags on abandoned rooftops. At night, the dogs of both sides barked through the dark, as though when their masters rested they took up the fight and yapped at one another till morning.
—Amos Elon, writing of the years when Jerusalem was divided by barbed wire

Evidence of the divided culture of Jerusalem's residents is easy to spot. Jewish men shop for souvenirs in the Old City *(top)*, while Arabs go about their daily business in the city's Arab section *(right)*.

A Divided City

I mmediately following the Six-Day War, the fence separating the Arab and Jewish sections of Jerusalem came down. But even in modern times, most Muslim Arabs and Jews continue to work and live in separate parts of Jerusalem. Both Arabic and Hebrew are official languages. The Muslim Arabs read Arabic newspapers, and the Israelis pick up Hebrew newspapers. Each side of the city has its own downtown business and entertainment districts.

The main business section in West Jerusalem is almost entirely Jewish. The Old City, in East Jerusalem, is almost entirely Arab. Welfare policies in the two sections are handled differently. Each side maintains its own fire departments, hospitals, and medical emergency crews. Schools are entirely separate. Two different bus systems travel the city, often following the same routes. Jews try to avoid using Muslim-controlled electric companies, and Arabs try to avoid using Israeli-owned banks. New roads make it possible for Israelis in Jerusalem's suburbs to travel back and forth almost without seeing a Muslim Arab.

In recent decades, the city's population has doubled. Since 1967 suburbs built for the growing Jewish population have tripled the size of the city. In West Jerusalem, new parks, theaters, concert halls, and museums have sprung up.

Israeli law gives the Arabs in Jerusalem full civil and cultural rights. Yet Arab Israelis don't have the same economic opportunities in modern-day Israel. Most land cannot legally pass out of Jewish control—even well-off Arab Israelis have a hard time buying property. Most Arab adults work on building sites, in restaurants, or on farms.

Because of its victory in the Six-Day War, Israel controls land that was formerly Palestine. Many Palestinians live under Israeli control in these occupied areas. The Intifada (a word meaning "to shake off") began in 1987. In this protest of Israel's control, some Israeli Arabs stopped paying taxes, threw stones at Israeli soldiers, and refused to give information to Israeli authorities. Palestinian terrorist groups, such as Hamas, have committed murder and planted bombs in public places. Israeli authorities arrested offenders and tightened security on camps in Israeli-occupied territory. At times, Israeli soldiers used violent methods to suppress the Intifada. The Intifada was not as active in Jerusalem as in other parts of Israel. Many Jewish and Arab people across Israel felt sorrow at the violence.

 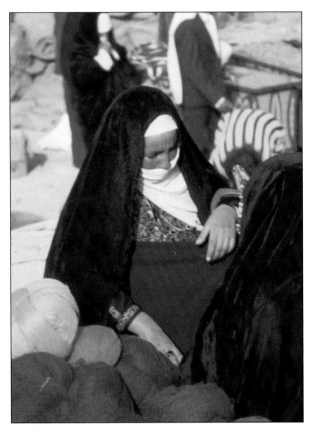

The Old City

*T*he Old City can be noisy. Church bells ring, donkeys carrying loads of goods bray, and the loudspeakers of mosques broadcast readings from the Koran. The stone walls surrounding the Old City contribute to the rich feeling of history. Young Israeli soldiers watch everyone who goes in or out of the Old City, their presence a reminder of the tensions in modern-day Jerusalem.

At sidewalk cafes, visitors enjoy the colorful streets of Jerusalem while basking in the mild Mediterranean climate, listening to street musicians, and sampling Middle Eastern food. Visitors from all over the world walk the narrow, stone-paved streets.

It's easy to spot the tourists from North America, Europe, Japan, or South America, who carry cameras and often wear T-shirts and jeans. In contrast, some Arab women wear shawls, veils, and long dresses—some exposing only their eyes. The women might balance baskets of vegetables and other goods on their heads as they walk home from the souk.

Hasidic Jewish men with beards and side curls wear black hats and long black

Impressions of Jerusalem's rich and turbulent history are everywhere—from pedestrians' traditional clothing styles and open display of religious devotion to the constant presence of soldiers in uniform.

coats. Other Jewish men don skull caps. Many Jewish Israelis and Muslim Arab men wear casual clothes. Armenian priests wear elaborate robes. Christian monks wear brown robes, and some nuns wear black habits. Some Christian ministers choose white collars.

The souk is packed with tiny stalls where merchants sell clothes, rugs, pots, and toys. Vendors sell tasty meat, fruit snacks, and souvenirs such as olive wood, crosses, prayer beads, and postcards.

The Western Wall is the remaining part of the Temple built by Herod the Great. It represents nearly four thousand years of Jewish history and is a powerful symbol of Judaism.

Each day, crowds of local residents and pilgrims come to the wall to pray, kiss the stones, and press into the cracks little pieces of paper with prayers written on them. The Western Wall is also considered part of the Dome of the Rock and the el-Aqsa Mosque on Temple Mount. Muslims believe that the wall is where the Prophet Muhammad tied his horse on his way to heaven.

Children in Jerusalem

The lives of Arab and Jewish children are similar in many ways. Jewish children attend religious schools, where they study history, language arts, science, math, Judaism, and English. They study the Torah and read Jewish literature.

Many Jewish families moved to Israel from places such as Russia, Germany, South Africa, Canada, Yemen, and the United States. Most kids learn how to speak Hebrew. Having a shared language helps Jewish people from all over the world speak with each other.

Some Arab children attend Muslim schools, where they study many of the same subjects as Jewish children. They read the Koran and learn about Islam. They speak Arabic instead of Hebrew.

Most children in Jerusalem walk to school after eating breakfast. Kids carry backpacks heavy with their books and bag lunches. Along the way, they pass crowds of the many different people who live in Jerusalem.

Children in Jerusalem like to watch American cartoons and movies with Hebrew subtitles. Some youngsters hope to study in the United States after high school. They like to discuss the latest local radio and television news with their friends.

Many children in the Old City like to play on the massive walls that still surround this section of the city. They race around, look for hidden treasures, or watch the new construction in the newer parts of the city. Ancient history is all around them. Some kids are lucky enough to find an artifact from the distant past as they explore.

Children in Jerusalem enjoy in-line skating after school *(opposite)* and jumping rope on school playgrounds *(left)*. A Jewish boy *(below)* perches on a ledge overlooking the Western Wall.

The Rhythm of Life

Jerusalem hums with the rhythms of interwoven lives and cultures. Five times each day, the mosques' loudspeakers call Muslims to prayer. Muslims throughout the city lay down prayer rugs to face Mecca, Islam's holiest city. Every afternoon, the bell of a Russian Orthodox church clangs to announce services. On Thursdays, the halal Arab markets are busy as Muslims prepare for their holy day of rest on Friday. On Fridays, the kosher Jewish markets are busy as Jews prepare for the Jewish Sabbath, which is on Saturday. On Fridays, Christians crowd the Via Dolorosa, and on Sundays they attend church.

On Thursdays and Saturdays, Jewish Bar Mitzvah parties gather at the Western Wall. Muslims, Jews, and Christians hold their annual festivals in the city. Almost every month, one group or another celebrates an ancient religious tradition.

Jerusalem houses some great treasures in its museums. One museum exhibits Islamic art. Another holds the Dead Sea Scrolls, the oldest existing copy of the Hebrew Bible. The Yad Va'shem Museum contains heart-wrenching exhibits about the experiences of Holocaust victims. Despite the tensions between Jerusalem's different faiths and cultures, this famous city is an important world capital.

Jerusalem gleams golden in the afternoon sun (above left). Jewish grandfathers (far left) offer up public prayers, while Arab women carry goods on their heads (left). The succulent smells of the marketplace (right) attract throngs of shoppers into their colorful interiors.

Jerusalem Timeline

	First Millennium B.C.	First Millennium A.D.

3000 B.C.–332 B.C. **Ancient History**	**C.3000 B.C.**	Powerful kingdom of Egypt begins
	C.2000 B.C.	First mention of Jerusalem recorded by Egyptians
	C.1250 B.C.	Moses leads the Israelites out of Egypt
	C.1200 B.C.	Phoenicians invent alphabet
	C.1000 B.C.	David captures Jerusalem and makes it the capital of his kingdom (uniting the tribes of Judah and Israel), and brings the Ark of the Covenant to the city
	C.965–928 B.C.	King Solomon's years of rule; he builds the first Temple
	722–701 B.C.	Assyrians destroy Israel, but Jerusalem survives a long siege
	597 B.C.	Babylonians (under King Nebuchadnezzar) conquer Jerusalem; most of the population is exiled
	539 B.C.	The Persian Empire (under King Cyrus) conquers Babylon; Cyrus encourages exiled people to return to their homes
	445 B.C.	A second, less dazzling Temple is built
332 B.C.–A.D. 571 **Greek and Roman Times**	**332 B.C.**	Alexander the Great makes Judea part of his Greek Empire
	63 B.C.	The Roman Empire (under General Pompey) captures Jerusalem
	37–4 B.C.	Herod the Great is king of Judah and builds a magnificent third Temple
	A.D. 33	Trial and crucifixion of Jesus
	A.D. 66	The Jews of Jerusalem openly rebel against Rome
	A.D. 70	Roman soldiers (led by Titus) crush the rebels, destroying Jerusalem and the Temple
	A.D. 132	The Roman emperor Hadrian offends the Jews and they rebel again; Hadrian defeats the rebels and bans the Jews from Jerusalem
	A.D. 135–326	Romans rename Jerusalem Aelia Capitolina
	A.D. 313	Constantine declares that Christianity is an accepted religion of the Roman Empire
A.D. 571–1517 **The Middle Ages**	**A.D. 571**	Muhammad is born in Mecca
	A.D. 638	Jerusalem falls under Muslim rule, peacefully conquered by Omar, Muhammad's successor
	A.D. 691	The Dome of the Rock is completed

A.D. 571–1517 The Middle Ages	A.D. 1099	The first Crusaders arrive in Jerusalem
	A.D. 1187	Saladin drives the Crusaders from Jerusalem
	A.D. 1260	The Mamluks of Egypt take control of the Islamic Empire and make many improvements in Jerusalem
A.D. 1517–1869 The Ottoman Era	A.D. 1517	The Ottoman Turks take control of the Muslim Empire, including Jerusalem
	A.D. 1520–66	The Ottoman sultan Süleyman makes many magnificent improvements in Jerusalem
	A.D. 1800s	Jerusalem becomes a focus of European interest and building projects
	A.D. 1869	A new road between Jaffa and Jerusalem is completed
	LATE 1800s	Zionists urge Jews to move to Palestine
A.D. 1869– Modern Jerusalem	A.D. 1917	A British document, the Balfour Declaration, favors giving Palestine to the Jews
	A.D. 1920	The British are given a mandate to rule Palestine
	A.D. 1939–1945	World War II and the Holocaust occur
	A.D. 1947	The British give up their mandate; the UN takes charge, dividing Palestine into two sections and making Jerusalem an international city
	A.D. 1948	State of Israel declared
	A.D. 1948–1967	Jerusalem is divided by barbed wire
	A.D. 1967	The Six-Day War occurs; Israel defies the UN by expanding its territory and declaring Jerusalem its capital
	A.D. 1987	The Intifada begins
	A.D. 1991	Peace talks between Israel, Syria, Lebanon, and a joint Jordanian-Palestinian delegation begin
	A.D. 1993	Israel and the PLO (Palestinian Liberation Organization) officially recognize each other
	A.D. 1994	Palestine begins to administer parts of the West Bank and Gaza Strip
	A.D. 1995	Israel's prime minister, Yitzak Rabin, is assassinated
	A.D. 2000	The future of Jerusalem discussed at Camp David summit

Books about Israel and Jerusalem

Ashabranner, Brent, and Gavriel and Jemal Ashabranner. *Two Boys of Jerusalem*. New York: Dodd, Mead & Company, 1984.

Bacon, Josephine. *Cooking the Israeli Way*. Minneapolis: Lerner Publications Company, 1986.

Biel, Timothy Levi. *The Age of Feudalism*. San Diego: Lucent Books, 1994.

Finkelstein, Norman H. *Theodore Herzel: Architect of a Nation*. Minneapolis: Lerner Publications Company, 1987.

Gresko, Marcia S. *Israel (Globe-trotters Club)*. Minneapolis: Carolrhoda Books, Inc., 2000.

Grossman, Laurie. *The Children of Israel*. Minneapolis: Carolrhoda Books, Inc., 2001.

Haas, Gerda. *Tracking the Holocaust*. Minneapolis: Runestone Press, 1995.

Israel in Pictures. Minneapolis: Lerner Publications Company, 1992.

Khalidi, Walid. *Before Their Diaspora: A Photographic History of the Palestinians 1876-1948*. Washington, D.C.: Institute for Palestine Studies, 1991.

Long, Cathryn J. *The Middle East in Search of Peace*. Brookfield, CT: Millbrook Press, 1994.

Macdonald, Fiona. *A 16th-Century Mosque*. New York: Peter Bedrick Books, 1994.

Nardo, Don. *Life on a Medieval Pilgrimage*. San Diego: Lucent Books, 1996.

Penney, Sue. *Islam. Discovering Religions Series*. Austin, TX: Raintree Steck-Vaughn, 1997.

Pirotta, Saviour. *Jerusalem: Holy Cities Series*. New York: Dillon, 1993.

Rogerson, John. *The Bible: Cultural Atlas for Young People*. New York: Facts on File, 1993.

Shamir, Ilana, ed. *The Young Reader's Encyclopedia of Jewish History*. New York: Viking, 1987.

Tubb, Jonathan N. *Bible Lands*. New York: Alfred A. Knopf, 1991.

Wolf, Bernard. *If I Forget Thee O Jerusalem*. New York: Dutton, 1998.

Index

About the Author and Illustrator

Diane Slavik is a writer who lives in Chicago with her husband, Steve Cory, and their three children. Her studies of world religions have led her to appreciate the treasures of history to be found in Jerusalem.

Ray Webb of Woodstock, England, studied art and design at Birmingham Polytechnic in Birmingham, England. A specialist in historical and scientific subjects, his work has been published in Great Britain, the Netherlands, Germany, and the United States. He continues to teach and lecture and especially enjoys introducing illustration as a career opportunity.

Acknowledgments
For quoted material: p. 16, *New American Standard Bible.* (Grand Rapids, Michigan: Zondervan Publishing House, 1999); pp. 19, 23, 28, C. K. Barrett. *The New Testament Background: Selected Documents.* (San Francisco: Harper & Row, 1956); p. 37, Timothy Levi Biel. *The Age of Feudalism.* (Lucent Books: San Diego, 1994); p. 39, Don Nardo. *Life on a Medieval Pilgrimage.* (San Diego: Lucent, 1996); pp. 46, 51, Amos Elon. *Battlegrounds of Memory.* (New York: Kodansha Globe, 1995); p. 49, Karen Armstrong. *Jerusalem: One City, Three Faiths.* (New York, Alfred A. Knopf, 1996).

For photographs and art reproductions: Tony Stone Images: (© Richard Passmore, p. 4), (© Paul Chesley, p. 55 left), (© Sarah Stone, p. 58 top), (© George Chan, p. 58 bottom left), (© Vince Streano, p. 59); Historical Picture Archive/CORBIS, p. 10 (top); Jewish Museum, New York/SuperStock, pp. 10 (bottom), 16 (top), 26 (bottom); The Granger Collection, pp. 16 (bottom), 18; Museo del Prado, Madrid/Bridgeman Art Library/SuperStock, p. 19; Mary Evans Picture Library, pp. 34, 39, 40; Brooklyn Museum of Art, New York, USA/Bridgeman Art Library, pp. 22-23, 26 (top); SuperStock, p. 28; Ospedale del Ceppo, Pistoia, Italy/Bridgeman Art Library, p. 31 (top); Bibliothèque Municipale de Lyon, France/Bridgeman Art Library, p. 31 (bottom); Christie's Images/SuperStock, pp. 32, 35; Bibliothèque Nationale, Paris, France/ Bridgeman Art Library, p. 37; Stock Montage, Inc., p. 38; Stapleton Collection, UK/Bridgeman Art Library, p. 41; The Fine Art Society, London, UK/ Bridgeman Art Library, p. 46; Archive Photos: (© Scott Swanson, p. 47), (Archive France/Tallandier, pp. 48, 50), (Warren Lieb, p. 52 bottom), (© Neil Strassberg, p. 57 bottom); Liaison Agency: (© Hulton Getty, pp. 49, 51), (© Serge Attal, p. 56); Panos Pictures: (© Caroline Penn, p. 52 top), (© Howard Davies, p. 57 top); © Albatross/Israel Ministry of Tourism, pp. 52 (center), 54 (right), 58 (bottom right); Panos Pictures: pp. 54 (left), 55 (right). Cover: © Buddy Mays/TRAVEL Stock.